SCHOLASTIC
News
Nonfiction Readers®

P9-DNF-933

Meet President Barack Obama

By Laine Falk

Children's Press®
An Imprint of Scholastic Inc.
New York Toronto London Auckland Sydney
Mexico City New Delhi Hong Kong
Danbury, Connecticut

These content vocabulary word builders are for grades 1–2

Subject Consultant: Eli J. Lesser, MA, Director of Education, National Constitution Center, Philadelphia, Pennsylvania

Reading Consultant: Cecilia Minden-Cupp, PhD, Early Literacy Consultant and Author, Chapel Hill, North Carolina

Photographs © 2009: AP Images: 13 (Obama for America), back cover, 7, 9 (Obama Presidential Campaign), 11 main (Lucy Pemoni), 11 inset (Punahou Schools); Aurora Photos/Callie Shell: 1, 15; Corbis Images/Wally McNamee: 22, 23; Getty Images: 2, 17 (Marvin E. Newman), 20, 21 (Marc Piscotty/Congressional Quarterly); Reuters/Jason Reed: 5; Courtesy of the U.S. Senate: cover foreground, 19; VEER/Jim Barber/Solus Photography: cover background.

Series Design: Simonsays Design!
Art Direction, Production, and Digital Imaging: Scholastic Classroom Magazines

Library of Congress Cataloging-in-Publication Data

Falk, Laine, 1974-
Meet President Barack Obama / Laine Falk.
    p. cm. — (Scholastic news nonfiction readers)
    Includes bibliographical references and index.
    ISBN 13: 978-0-531-23403-7 (lib. bdg.)   978-0-531-23524-9 (pbk.)
    ISBN 10: 0-531-23403-7 (lib. bdg.)   0-531-23524-6 (pbk.)
    1. Obama, Barack—Juvenile literature. 2. Presidents—United States—Biography—Juvenile literature. 3. Presidential candidates—United States—Biography—Juvenile literature.
    4. African American legislators—Biography—Juvenile literature. 5. Legislators—United States—Biography—Juvenile literature. 6. United States. Congress. Senate—Biography—Juvenile literature. 7. Racially mixed people—United States—Biography—Juvenile literature. I. Title. II. Series.
    E901.1.O23F34 2009
    328.73092—dc22   [B] 2008041383

CONTENTS

Pictures of Our President

Meet our new President. His name is Barack Obama [buh-ROK oh-BAH-muh]. Let's look at photos to learn about his life.

The American people voted to make Barack Obama President in 2008.

Here is Barack on the beach when he was little. He is with his grandfather.

The beach is in Hawaii. That is where Barack was born.

Pacific
Ocean

U.S.

Hawaii
(U.S.)

Can you find Barack in this photo of his family?

When Barack was 6, he and his mom moved. They went to another country. His sister, Maya, was born there.

His mom

His stepdad

Maya

Barack

Barack and his mom moved to Indonesia.

ASIA

U.S.

Pacific Ocean

Indonesia

AUSTRALIA

Here is Barack's high school. The school is in Hawaii. Barack moved back there when he was 10 years old.

He was a good student. He loved to play basketball.

This is Barack when he was in high school.

11

This photo shows Barack Obama as a teacher. Before he was President, he was a teacher and a lawyer. He was also a Senator [SEN-uh-tur]. A Senator helps make laws.

He lived in Chicago.

Illinois ⇒ ○Chicago

Chicago is a city in Illinois.

ON SELF INTEREST

Michelle is Barack Obama's wife. They have two girls. Malia is 10 years old. Sasha is 7. Both girls like to play tennis. They both play the piano.

Here is President Obama's family today.

Sasha

Malia

Michelle

When he became President, Barack Obama and his family moved. They moved into the White House! The White House is where the President lives and works.

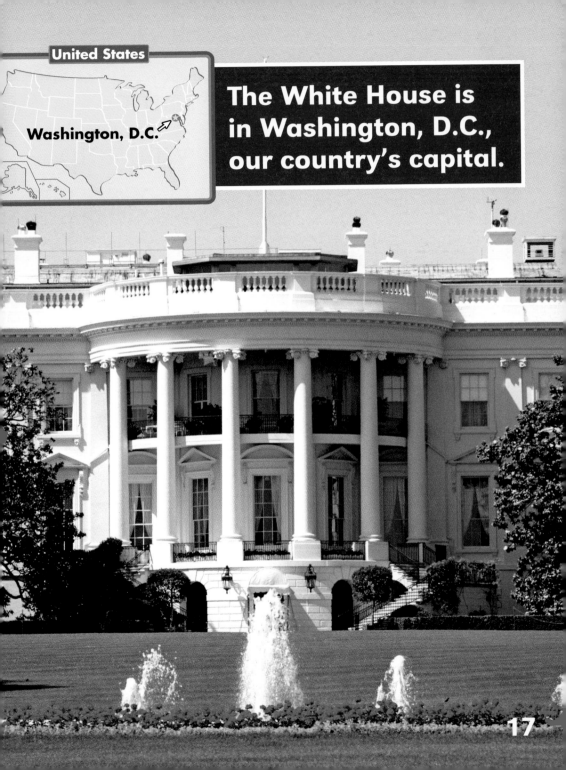

United States

Washington, D.C.

The White House is in Washington, D.C., our country's capital.

Now President Obama has a big job. He will help make laws that everyone must follow. He will help keep our country safe.

He will do his best to lead the United States of America.

Barack Obama is the 44th President of the United States.

At a big meeting in August 2008, Barack Obama was chosen to run for President.

In November 2008, the American people voted. Barack Obama won the election!

INAUGURATION DAY

On January 20, 2009, Barack Obama became President. He stood in front of the U.S. Capitol in Washington, D.C. He took an oath, or made a promise, to be a good President.

INDEX

FIND OUT MORE
Book:
Stier, Catherine. *If I Were President*. Morton Grove, Illinois: Albert Whitman & Company, 2004.

Website:
The White House
www.whitehouse.gov/kids

MEET THE AUTHOR
Laine Falk is a writer and Scholastic editor. She lives in Brooklyn, New York, with her family.